JOY AFTER
Failure
A Model for Decision Making

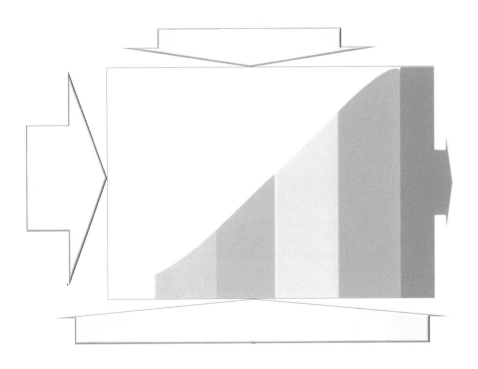

LINDA A BANKOSKI

WestBow Press books may be ordered through booksellers or by contacting:

WestBow Press
A Division of Thomas Nelson & Zondervan
1663 Liberty Drive
Bloomington, IN 47403
www.westbowpress.com
1 (866) 928-1240

ISBN: 978-1-9736-3700-4 (sc)
ISBN: 978-1-9736-3701-1 (e)

Library of Congress Control Number: 2018909661

Print information available on the last page.

WestBow Press rev. date: 02/06/2019

WESTBOW
PRESS®
A DIVISION OF THOMAS NELSON
& ZONDERVAN

CONTENTS

To my daughter, Leann, and the many dear sisters and brothers who have traveled this journey with me and given me wisdom, encouragement, love, and support. I hope you know who you are.

PREFACE

This book is based on my beliefs, experiences, and observations. I do not present anything here as facts or as the results of research. Some of it may resonate with you, my dear reader. Some of it may not. Feel free to disagree with me. I reserve the right to be wrong and to learn and change what I believe, and you have the right to do the same. If you find this to be helpful, please put it to use. If not, pass it along to someone else. We all have the opportunity to learn from our decisions. Someone once told me, "Everything is a lesson. Some lessons are just more expensive than others."

When the student is ready, the teacher will appear.

—Zen proverb

ACKNOWLEDGMENTS

Because this is the result of many years of effort, it is impossible to list all of the people who have helped me, encouraged me, offered suggestions, and supported me. My heart overflows with gratitude. Rather than slight someone, I will list just one. Many thanks to my dedicated editor, Laura N. Gasaway. Without her, this would never have become a reality.

CHAPTER 1

The Choice Cycle

The model in this book came to me in a dream. I have found it useful, and I believe it will be useful for all of us. I hope that you will be helped by it as I have been.

In the dream, I was in the talent competition of a famous beauty pageant. My talent was presenting the model that I am sharing with you here. In the dream, I was not allowed to use pictures or posters, and without the pictures, I found it next to impossible to share my talent. Yet I refused to leave the stage until everyone understood. No amount of coaxing and cajoling, even from my mother, would convince me to leave the stage.

So, what was it that was so compelling? I'm happy to tell you.

What I visualized was a model that I call the Choice Cycle. It is based on the *cost of quality,* which is a fairly common concept that businesses use for quality management. I believe that it can be much more than a way to calculate the financial impact of management decisions. I think of it as an economics model that anyone can use to manage resources. It can also be the basis to understand and influence many of our life decisions and to guide behavior to improve our lives. Many of us think in pictures rather than in words, so remembering the image of the Choice Cycle is very helpful.

I am a lifelong learner. This model has been my instruction manual for decisions I make and actions I take. I've used it as a road map to inform me where I've been. I've used it as a GPS to help me find my way, and I've used it as a mental bookshelf to catalog and store what I hear and learn. I have used it in real time—in the moment—and sometimes, when I reflect on the past, it helps me get a better understanding of what happened. What I am sharing with you is an evolved version. Because I use it daily to enlighten me, I have changed it too many times to count. It now represents more than thirty years of my experience and learning from using it.

In short, I have relied on the Choice Cycle to discover, recover, and maintain joy. My hope is that it will give you insight for your decisions.

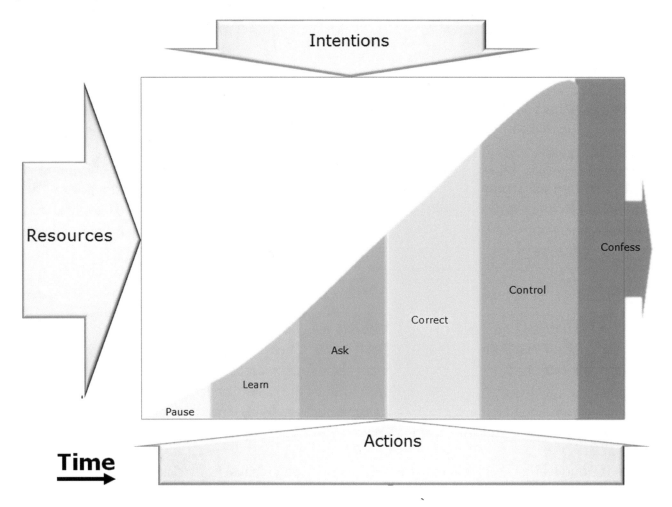

Whoa! Too much! Too busy! Too complex! Yes, it is. And what does all of this mean anyway? Let's unpack.

Start on the left side. We all have *resources*. Resources include things like friends, money, and education. My definition of resources is what we use to get what we want or need. Our resources are what we receive and accumulate over time. They are ours to use, invest, or waste as we choose.

On the bottom left is the word "time." That is a tricky one. In English, we use one word—time—whereas other languages use more words to express the concept of time. Now, I am not a linguist, and I hereby reserve the right to be wrong about this (and everything else you read here). In Greek and Latin, I understand that there are several words to describe time. Two of them are *horas* and *chronos.* From those sounds and root words, we get *hours* and *chronology.* Time comes to us moment by moment, in a chronological sequence. We use our time one unit at a time. We describe those units of time with many names, such as seconds, minutes, hours, days, weeks, months, years, decades, and lifetimes, and symbols, such as the dash between two dates on a gravestone.

We also can decide on our actions. The arrow at the bottom of the chart shows us the choices of actions that we can take. They are the decisions we make and the actions we take that consume our resources. Chronology is continual. There are opportunities arriving moment by moment, and they each use resources.

We can decide to pause and then learn. We can ask questions and then listen to the answers. Our next choice is to accept the result or, if we don't like the outcome, try to correct it. If we fail to "fix it," then we try to control the damage. When we have exhausted our resources or options, we are left with one decision, which is to admit that we have run out of resources. When we get to that point, in the next moment, the only decision is to confess failure and begin the cycle again with the hope of making better choices next time.

The colored bars in the middle represent the costs of the actions, and the arrow at the right leads to the next cycle. The cycle continues, and the opportunities to make choices about our actions repeat again and again.

The arrow at the top represents our intentions. It includes the things that we aim to do, standards we want to meet, and targets.

Often in the face of an opportunity, our first inclination is to consider what resources we have and what resources we need. A big aha moment came when I realized that the resources we have are actually the *consequences* of our choices and actions. What I have learned from using the Choice Cycle is that it is far better to decide based on what I value, intend, or plan rather than hoping or guessing that my resources will be enough.

Since better decisions are those made based on our intentions and plans rather than on our resources, we can pause and then decide and define what we intend to do and put together a "good enough" plan. It only needs to be *good enough* because we know that we have opportunities to learn and then decide on our actions. Next, we can move forward based on the results of our evaluation. We can decide to be self-controlled and self-disciplined and stay focused on our intentions. We can identify and keep our eyes on the prize. Remember that the resources we have are the consequences of our ability to make sound decisions and take meaningful actions.

We are fortunate to live in an abundant universe. There is enough for all of us. There are no resource problems, just priority and distribution problems. In finance, there is a term used as a measure of performance or a way to compare investments. It's called return on investment (ROI). What we invest our resources in will be returned in one form or another—a return on our intentions and a return on our investments. That is the ROI of life.

Whether it is yours or mine, life really is a talent show. Every *now* ushers in the next moment, and every moment offers us an opportunity to choose how we will act and how we will live. When we fail, it is just a call to wake up and joyfully begin again. Some of my greatest failures have been the lead into some of my greatest joys. It is my joy to share what I have learned along the way so that you too will discover the joy that follows challenging times: the joy after failure.

CHAPTER 2

Resources—What You Have

In chapter 1, I mentioned that I have found it helpful to know that resources are most often the results or consequences of my decisions. The better the choices, the more resources I have.

When we say "resources," most people immediately think of money, time, and the number of people available. Those are only some of the resources we have available to us. Resources are often what we love. Resources are both tangible and intangible. We can describe resources in six primary categories: human, money, time, stuff, relationships, and unique.

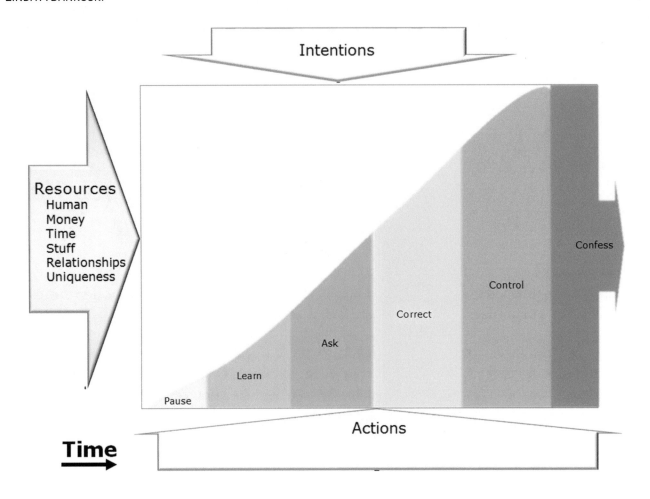

Human Resources

In the category of human resources, there are four types of resources that people possess. People bring their energy, skills, knowledge, and expertise. These resources are valuable. Failure to recognize or acknowledge our energy, skills, knowledge, or expertise does not diminish their value. It just makes resources more inaccessible. It is like having a savings account you don't realize you have.

Many times, we have heard someone declare, "People are our most valuable resource." Sadly, we see that decisions and actions often tell a different story. Agreements can be made and broken. Too often, we offer our assets in situations that do not value those assets.

Humans bring renewable resources—perhaps the only truly renewable resource. To renew our energy, sometimes it is as simple as changing our thoughts. Better thoughts or different perspectives have an immediate impact on human energy. Human energy is vital fuel. We may think of human energy as spirit.

For example, in selecting people to be part of a team to work with me on a project, I have a choice. If I can choose from three people who are excited to work on the project and ten people who don't care, I will happily choose the three people. Likewise, if I have to choose from three people who know what they need to know and ten who don't, I'll choose the three. It is because the number of people is not as important as the energy, skills, knowledge, and expertise that they bring and their willingness to contribute. Because they can be counted, people are tangible, but what they contribute is intangible.

We value the people who have or who give freely from their assets.

Money

When someone asks, "Do you have the resources?" one of the first thoughts is often money. In fact, for some people, money and resources are synonymous. From my experiences, when decisions are made based *only* on money, they often turn out to be bad.

The money we have is generally based on what we traded for it. We trade our time for money when we work in paid positions. We trade our stuff for money when we sell something we own. We trade our time for expertise or knowledge. Some people exchange money for education, while others invest their time in the school of hard knocks. Money is typically a medium of exchange for other resources. Although money is symbolic for value, we usually think of it as tangible.

Time

Time is the most equitable of our resources because we each have exactly the same amount—twenty-four hours each day. What we don't know is how many of those twenty-four-hour units we have, and we can never know that. We may hear people say that they didn't have time to do something, but the reality is that they are offering an excuse for how they used their twenty-four hours, the moments they have now. Allocation of the twenty-four hours that we have is a decision. We might use it or waste it. Every minute of every day is either spent or invested. The problem is not a lack of time. The problem is the priorities. We might be able to measure it, but time is intangible.

Time is an extremely valuable resource. It is sometimes called our most precious resource.

Stuff

Some people love their stuff! Stuff or our belongings are the physical things that we acquire and call our own. Houses, cars, equipment, clothes, inventory—the list goes on and on. For many of us, it would not even be possible to list the all of the stuff that we say is ours. We can choose to sell it, give it away, throw it away, or keep it. If we keep it, we then make decisions to use it, store it, move it, or maintain it. In other words, we use our other resources to manage it. Because of its physical nature, stuff is clearly tangible.

Relationships

Another resource available to us is our relationships. We may have relationships with friends, family, supporters, fans, or colleagues. Relationships are connections. They are sometimes called our support group or network, which describes connections. Our relationships may be close, distant, or virtual. Typically, our relationships are based on shared experiences, history, beliefs, or bonds. Our belief in a relationship that we trust gives us energy. When we have a need, it may be our relationships that we call on to help fill that need. Relationships are intangible.

Unique

In addition to all of these resources, each of us also has other intangible resources. We each have such things as health, faith, a reputation, technologies, proprietary information, and influence that are unique to us. Individuals and organizations may use their unique resources without even realizing that it is a resource until it is threatened. Our good name is largely invisible to us until it is at risk. For example, a company may build a brand image and will take legal action against others who attempt to steal or imitate or damage that image. They may also spend huge sums to improve their corporate image or to combat negative comments. In the age of social media, the depletion of our resources may happen before we are aware of it. Organizations and individuals rely on their uniqueness to accomplish their tasks and goals. It is helpful to recognize and value what makes us unique.

The value of resources is often based on understanding. In the fable *The Emperor's New Clothes*,[1] the emperor hired weavers to make him new clothes that only competent people would be able to see. Although the emperor could not see the clothes, he didn't want to admit it because that would mean that he was incompetent. He marched out, acting as if he was covered. He believed that no one would know that he couldn't see the clothes. He also believed that he would be able to identify those around him who were incompetent. Everything was fine until a child pointed out that the emperor had no clothes. Indeed, the emperor was exposed because he behaved as if he had resources that he did not have. As long as everyone was in agreement regarding what they saw, the emperor's reputation was intact.

Understanding the value of resources changes based on beliefs and needs. Money (paper and coins), time (cost or price/hour), people (value of skills and knowledge), tangible items (utility), and intangible things may seem worthless to one person and valuable to another. We use our resources to fund what we choose to do. Like most investments, our decisions result in either more or fewer resources.

Sometimes we fail to account for our resources. I have found it valuable to take an inventory of resources. It gives me a better perspective and can often be instrumental in shifting my beliefs and attitude. It also helps me create better plans that result in getting the resources I need.

On the next few pages is a worksheet to account for your inventory and plan changes. Don't worry about the accuracy of the inventory. It is a snapshot of how you think about your resources now. If you think of yourself as "poor," it can help you identify the areas in which you believe there is a lack.

---
[1] Hans Christian Andersen.

Resource Inventory

For each category of resource, put an X on the line where you think you are today. Mark an O where you need or want to be.

Human (Energy, Knowledge, Skills, Ability)

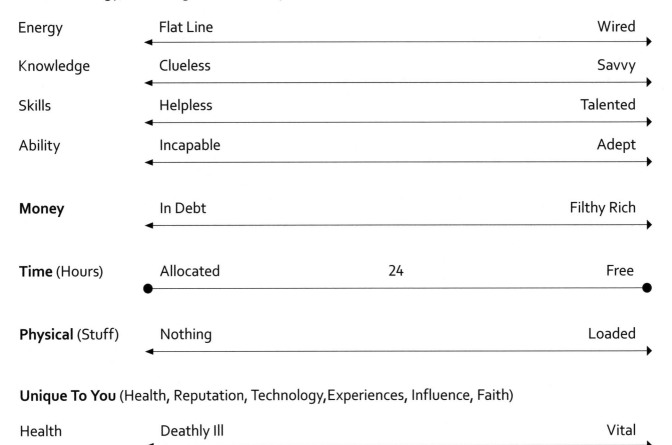

Energy	Flat Line	Wired
Knowledge	Clueless	Savvy
Skills	Helpless	Talented
Ability	Incapable	Adept

Money — In Debt — Filthy Rich

Time (Hours) — Allocated — 24 — Free

Physical (Stuff) — Nothing — Loaded

Unique To You (Health, Reputation, Technology, Experiences, Influence, Faith)

Health	Deathly Ill	Vital
Reputation	Trashed	Impeccable
Technology	Restricted	Unlimited

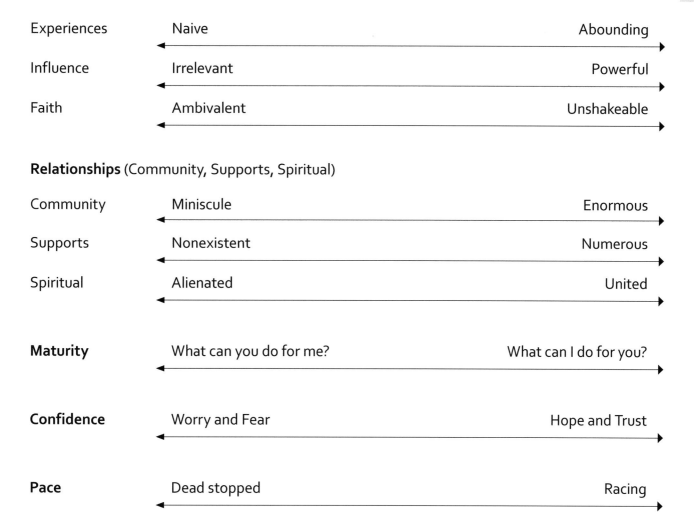

Experiences	Naive	Abounding
Influence	Irrelevant	Powerful
Faith	Ambivalent	Unshakeable

Relationships (Community, Supports, Spiritual)

Community	Miniscule	Enormous
Supports	Nonexistent	Numerous
Spiritual	Alienated	United

Maturity	What can you do for me?	What can I do for you?
Confidence	Worry and Fear	Hope and Trust
Pace	Dead stopped	Racing

Circle each category where there is a gap between the X and the O. Decide what you would like your target to be. Use the next page to write an action plan to move toward the target.

Actions I will take	By when (date)	**D**one or **P**lan?

It is very helpful to get an overview of resources to visualize and clarify priorities. I've found the worksheet useful to recognize patterns in my behavior. Are my resources out of balance?

For example, if we are loaded with stuff, it may require more time and money to maintain it than we are willing to spend. Likewise, if we are deathly ill, we may need to depend on relationships, and a lot of stuff might be a burden. If someone who depends on us for support puts themselves at risk, we may not have enough influence to help them.

If we are satisfied with the balance of our resources, the decision is to continue the status quo. If we want different resources, then it will take changing the way we make decisions.

Without an inventory and an action plan, we can fool ourselves with what we say. We can start believing that we don't have money. Rather than saying, "I can't afford it," I may say, "That is not the way I want to spend my money." I once looked in my purse and found two coins. I decided that I would make them last for a week. It was easier to make decisions with a clear priority. It would have been a lie to say that I had no money. Replacing negative words with positive words can keep us from feeling stuck. Make decisions, not excuses.

A written action plan is a way to hold ourselves accountable. It is more likely that I will fulfill a commitment or start something new with an actual plan. It is a natural inclination to be vague. For example, which of the following will more likely result in lunch? "Let's get together for lunch sometime," or "Let's get together for lunch on Tuesday at noon in the café"? Action plans can create momentum. Changing a plan is easier than getting started. A parked car cannot be steered in a new direction. We need to keep moving and adjusting as we go.

Hope is a poor strategy. To change old habits and live more intentionally, it takes making different choices. In chapter 3, we will look at decisions and how to make good choices.

Decisions—What You Do

Not all of our decisions must be made at one time, and we don't get all of our time at once. It is human nature to want to control some things. Much of what happens around us is not within our control. What we can control is our thoughts, our attitudes, our decisions, and our actions. We also have control of the units of resources that we choose to spend or invest for what we want or need to do. Time comes to us moment by moment, and in each moment, we have opportunities to decide what we will do. The chart below shows that there is an order in which opportunities arrive.

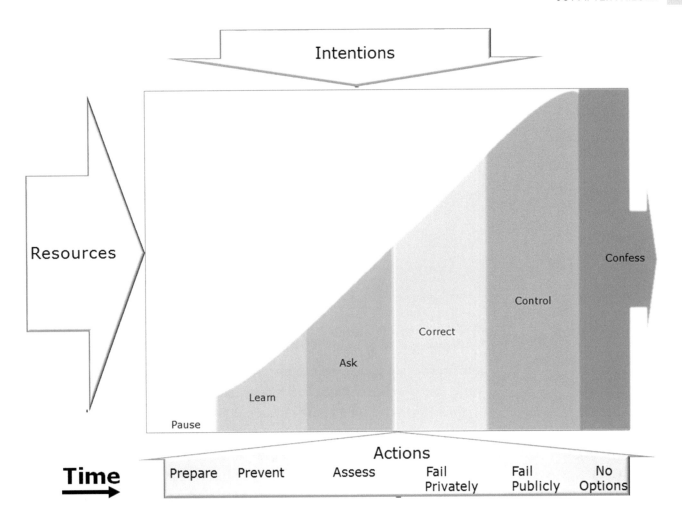

Actions

The choices of our actions range from pausing to prepare to confessing that there are no options left. I've used colors to signify the different choices. The color for pausing is white, signifying peace. The color for learning is green, to signify growth. The color for asking is blue, to signify openness and inquisitiveness. The color for correcting is yellow, to signify caution, and the color for controlling is red, to signify danger. The color for confessing and the lack of further actions is gray, signifying gloom and doom.

Fear can be a barrier to taking appropriate action. Sometimes we get stuck if we believe that we don't have significant knowledge or the risks are too high.

There are few stories of people dedicated to calm and peace, and there are many stories of people scrambling in the face of crisis. Stillness is not the same as stagnant. Taking action is setting something into motion. Common expressions about not taking appropriate actions are "shooting from the hip" or "going off half-cocked." It is interesting that both refer to the poor use of a weapon. Our resources are our weapons to use well or not so well.

Prepare

The first choice we have to make is whether or not to prepare. The key word is *pause*. For most of us, the primary action required is to decide to do it and take time to slow down and be still. It is an invitation to quiet the mind and body. If we pause, we can become centered and clarify our thoughts, and consider what we want to do and how we want to act. Major religious traditions refer to pausing by names such as meditation, centering, mindfulness, prayer, serenity, devotions, Sabbath, and so on. Regularly scheduled practices, such as yoga, improve practitioners' lives. Simply taking a deep breath can be valuable. In fact, with every breath, there is a built-in pause. Inhale, pause, exhale, pause. Walking also includes pauses. Step, pause as our weight shifts, step. We can become conscious of the pauses. During the pause, we are refilled, refreshed, renewed, and recreated. In school, we had recesses. It is the time when we make deposits in our bank of resources. We decide or discover our true intentions and can plan to do things accordingly when we pause and refuel.

It isn't really obvious that pausing is a choice, but it is. If our habit is being busy and running, we may not even notice that we made a choice to not pause. Choosing to pause is not necessarily sitting down and meditating. There are occasions when making that choice is easy. It is so easy that we don't even realize that we made a choice. In an emergency, we make the choice with no thought at all. It is not a conscious choice but rather is taking action based on previous experience, anticipated consequences, or what we value.

If we choose to pause and prepare, the cost is very small. We spend less than one unit of our resources. We invest in our lives and our future. It is the opportunity we take to get the priorities clear. Chapter 4 will describe in greater detail the rules we can choose that are important to us.

Of course, in our fast-paced lives, we often choose not to pause and prepare.

Prevent

The next choice offers the opportunity to prevent failures. The key words/action of prevention are *learn and think*. We can choose to use our resources to discover, read, study, and absorb.

It may require the involvement of others, or it may be a solitary task. Some of us may use the writings of sages, literature, journals, or some other favorite source of guidance, wisdom, truth, lessons, instructions, or inspiration. Others may use holy scriptures. What is important is that we invest the time to learn from the resources of others and to be inspired.

It is common to hear adults speak about the importance of education, yet those same adults may not have a routine practice of intentional learning. When we listen to what others believe or know, we may not agree with everything they say. What we gain, however, is a different perspective. When we learn about what others know or believe, we can sift through and find what aligns with our perspective and what does not. Either way, the value is in our choice to take advantage of the energy, skills, knowledge, and expertise of others because they are willing to share with us. Chapter 8 offers more information about perspectives.

Learning is essential for growth and to avoid pitfalls and problems. It is also allows us to reflect on the past. We can think about what lessons we need to learn, what matters to us, and what our priority is, and we can try to understand what happened in the past and consider what we need for the future we want.

Choosing to learn will prevent future problems. One of the problems with prevention is that it is impossible to know the true value of prevention because we can't ever prove what didn't happen. Some action must be taken to avoid being stuck. Taking no action is sometimes called paralysis by analysis.

Focusing on prevention is making an investment in ourselves and the future, and it will cost us more of our resources. Let's call it one unit.

It is very common to think of the decisions to prepare and prevent as unimportant. In fact, because they take few resources, there is a tendency to decide to skip them and dive right in. The small investment that is required is worth far more than it seems. One of the challenges is to even remember that it really is a decision to think and learn. It might just be thinking ahead of what could go wrong or what needs to be right. It might be worthwhile to resolve to take a deep breath before diving in. It's similar to swimming. Eventually, we have to take the plunge or at least get our feet wet.

Assess

Next is the opportunity to be open and check the status of where we are and the potential risks. We pay attention. We observe, take stock, count, measure, and evaluate. One thing to assess is our self-talk because it can deplete or maintain our resources like energy. The key word is *ask*, and implied in asking is *listening*. The assessment can be auditory or silent observation. It is an investment that serves to increase our resources, such as resources of energy, skills, knowledge, expertise, and relationships. Listening is one of the most empowering activities we can undertake. It energizes because it is an indication that we were heard. It is even more energizing when we can see a positive impact. At the conclusion of an assessment, we can evaluate whether the results met our expectations. Satisfaction occurs when the expectation and what actually happened match. Because perfection is difficult to achieve, there is often some element of dissatisfaction. Things are not often black or white, or pass/fail. So, we can celebrate what went according to plan and identify what did not. It is the determination of shades of gray. When the result includes some amount of dissatisfaction, we feel energy decrease. When we realize that we have exceeded our expectations, we are reenergized and feel good about what we have accomplished. Assessment is related to learning yet typically involves investing more resources. Let's assume that this choice takes two units of our resources.

Not assessing is also a choice. If we choose, we can decide not to do any assessment. We can take a chance, take risks, or rely on luck. Sometimes that works out. Often, the decision to test and evaluate is based on what is at stake or what resources we are willing to risk. Gamblers are successful sometimes, and often the best gamblers are actually good at assessing situations. If successful, that builds resources. Lack of success is sometimes called failure.

Fail Privately

What comes next is private failure. Private failure is a failure that only you know about. It is when we discover that there are problems or things we should have or could have done and didn't do them. It is self-inflicted pain. Sometimes it is conscious, and sometimes it is unconscious, but we know. Deep down, we know. When we acknowledge that everything is not okay or become aware that something is not satisfactory, our first response to ourselves is usually, "Oh no!" We want desperately to deny the failure. We don't want to believe it. We may even pretend it isn't true. We may say that it isn't true. We may even try to hide it or lie. We may try without much success to "unknow it." When we discover that there is a problem, it feels like a failure. It is what it is, and we eventually have to admit it to ourselves. The key word is *correct*. In that moment, we try to think of what we can or should do to fix the failure or avoid exposure. It won't go away no matter how much we wish and desire that.

A common response to the recognition of failure is to search for the cause or find something or someone to blame. We think about what should have or could have been done. We want to make every effort to avoid feeling that we failed. Denying, blaming, delaying, and avoiding do nothing to remedy the problem. The last thing we want, however, is the feeling of helplessness. We don't want to acknowledge that we will have to do something to correct the problem. To fix it will take resources dedicated to correction. We wait and hope that no one will find out. We don't mind the problem as much as we mind that someone else might know about it. For example, we might not mind living in a space that is not neat or clean, but when we learn that visitors are coming, we clean and straighten up. We take control and do what we can do. Sometimes it is only to hide the evidence of the problem because we want to look good and save ourselves from embarrassment.

Private failures are an impending publicly known failure. It is just a matter of time before it is out of our control. How we handle failure defines our character. We must forgive ourselves.

Once we understand that there is a problem that needs our attention, it will take about five times the resources to address the problem.

Fail Publicly

Public failure is when our worst fears come true, and someone or everyone knows. We realize that the evidence can no longer be hidden. Our choices are to deny what is obvious or to readily admit the reality. When we choose to deny what is visible and known, we embarrass ourselves further and simply delay the inevitable. In time, the whole truth is revealed. Well-known politicians and religious people are clear examples of learning this the hard way. In his farewell address on January 9, 2017, President Obama warned, "Reality has a way of catching up with you."

This type of failure is known by many names, such as tragedy, disaster, catastrophe, debacle, or fiasco. There comes a moment when we know, and "they" know—when we receive the letter, the phone call, the message, the notice, the announcement, or the report. We refer to those moments as a single moment. We usually say "the" because it becomes public or known in a single moment. There is before and after. We can usually remember exact details about where we were and when we learned that the failure had become public.

If we admit the reality of the situation, we begin trying to control the damage. When we deny the problem, we delay taking control of what we can and waste more resources. Let it hurt. The key word is *control*.

With social media, it has become much more difficult to keep problems private and much more expensive to do damage control. When we have used the resources that we are willing to use, or we don't have access to any additional resources, we stop the efforts to control. If we believe that we have unlimited resources, we remain in the control mode. We can sometimes see this with wealthy and famous people or politicians who believe they have enough resources (money, influence, and reputation) to avoid admitting the problem.

Examples of public failure are everywhere. They may be personal or in business, politics, or religion. They are usually seen in headlines and very memorable events. They are the defining moments, turning points, hallmarks, and "I remember when" moments. The expenditure of resources is anywhere from ten units to infinity.

No Options

The point at which nothing more can be done and the excuses are rejected marks the end of the resources and the opportunities to choose. The key word is *confess*. We admit the failure to ourselves and to others.

It is when the madness and frantic activity stop. There are no further options other than to end it and accept the failure.

We hear or say words like "It's over" or "We did all we could do." When the situation is recognized for what it is, it results in regret and sorrow. There aren't any do-overs.

After the failures, there is an opportunity to shift to joy! We survived!

The key words are *next time*. A fresh start. It's the next moment, and we find ourselves beginning again. We have another opportunity, a second (or ten thousandth) chance to make choices. If we have used, spent, or expended our resources, it is a waste only if we fail to recognize that we actually just exchange our resources. If I use money, I may gain knowledge or a skill. If I lose my energy or health, what resource do I get in return? If I take a job, perhaps I am agreeing to exchange my resources of time, energy, and knowledge for money, skills, or relationships.

Someone once said, "Nothing is useless. It can always serve as a bad example," which is true if we make the choice to pause and learn before we begin our *next time*.

Guilt, regret, and comparisons to others sap our resources. They are self-punishment and of no value. We need to give ourselves permission to go through another cycle. We will repeat the cycle until we learn the lesson. Next time is an opportunity for self-improvement and less chaos. We begin the next time, and we learn to stop wasting resources. We stop burning bridges, squandering money, wasting time, and throwing stuff away. The question is, How many times will I have to fail before I learn?

Joy comes at the dawning of a new cycle when we recognize that there are new opportunities for success.

I heard a prayer once that I think is powerful. "Lord, for all that happened before this moment, thank you. And for everything that happens from now on, yes!" Awaken to joy! Joy begins the cycle again. We may feel excited or renewed. Our instincts, intuition, and feelings can be relied upon as guides to where we are in the cycle. When we finish pausing, we feel *peace*. Next is a chance to anticipate the possibilities, and we feel *curious*. When we are assessing, there is usually an *anxious* feeling. It is important to evaluate what is going on, both good and bad. If we choose to look at the what-ifs and acknowledge our vulnerability, we will begin to see our private failures and feel the *fear* that accompanies them. If we realize that our private failure is about to become public, the feeling is *panic*. And when we have used all of the resources and reserves that we have, we feel depleted and spent and then begin thinking about next time. I think our four most important words are *thank you* and *next time*. Then we remember to begin with joy and finally pause and learn, and we create a better future.

CHAPTER 4

Intentions and Plans—What Is Important

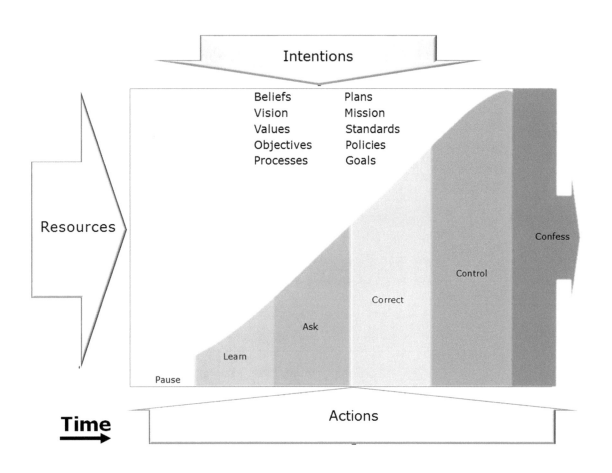

Intentions

Beliefs   Plans
Vision   Mission
Values   Standards
Objectives   Policies
Processes   Goals

Resources

Confess

Control

Correct

Ask

Learn

Pause

Time

Actions

Instructions and Rules

Our lives did not come with rules and instructions, yet they are critical to living a life of joy. In life, just as in most things, the more specific the instructions, the more valuable they are. So, where do we get the instructions and rules for our lives? When we are young, the rules are created and managed for us. We are thought to be good when we are disciplined to follow the established or imposed rules. I once heard a teen say, "I just figured out that in life, there are no rules." That isn't exactly true. As we mature, we gain more and more freedom to choose our own rules for how we live, and then we choose when and how they apply. We may still be called good, or perhaps we are called successful. Of course, some rules are established by the group or society in which we choose to live. For example, we might want to operate an automobile. To be allowed on public roadways, we must follow many rules, including speed limits, traffic signals, and road signs. We may decide to break them, and in that case, we may leave or be removed from participating in the group, society, or community. In the example of driving an automobile, failure to follow the rules can result in losing driving privileges. We also choose when our rules or behaviors need to change.

The beginning point of our personal rules is our intention. Choosing to live according to what we believe requires clear thoughts as well as self-discipline and self-control. A statement of intention is a description of how we wish to live. That may include plans, which are a strategy for doing something, standards, which is level of accomplishment, and objectives, which are steps to achieve goals—which are targets. Policies are rules of action, and processes are a series of activities. The definitions of these can be confusing and overlap. The point is to make decisions that will define success. It is our desired way of choosing to think and behave, and when we do that consistently and well, we may be called successful. For each of us, success is an inside job. To achieve success as a group, we hope that others will act and live in agreement with what we believe and think.

Intentions

Intentions are called by many titles, including purpose. Even at a very young age, children understand purpose. During play, when someone is hit by a ball, you can hear children say, "You did that on purpose," which is a statement of belief about the intention behind the action. In fact, purpose is the combination of intention and action. Intention without action has little practical value, as there is no result.

A formula could be stated as Purpose = Intention + Actions = Results.

A friend of mine is fond of saying, "Your system is designed to give you exactly the results that you are getting. If you want different results, you must change the system." A system is the complex, coordinated, interacting activities and functions involved in doing something. To be effective, a system needs a purpose, a method, and a way to measure results. Purpose is a powerful motivator. We might have a lot of know-how and have very little know-why. Purpose provides the "why," the method provides the "how, when, and where," and the measure of the result provides the "what." Without the why, our activities can feel meaningless. Without a method, it is just a wish or a dream, and without a measure, it is just a rehearsal in preparation for the real performance. Yet, as someone once said, "Life is not a rehearsal." Intentions are vows that we make to ourselves. They are promises we want to keep.

It is common to hear leaders, managers, and people in many walks of life talk about vision, missions, values, and principles. In fact, it is far easier to talk about them than to take the time and thoughtfully define them and understand how to use and evaluate them.

Vision

Vision is the desired glimpse of the future or the way for the future desire to become the reality. Vision is defined in words that create a compelling picture. A well-defined vision helps people see the future. When it is clear enough for people to see, smell, taste, feel, or hear the future, it energizes them to focus and work to make it a reality. Clear vision is powerful. It generates energy, a vital resource. If you can't see a desired future, you won't move forward to make it become a reality.

Look at pictures of an island with palm trees. If you were offered an all-expense-paid trip, would you want to go? Why? Because you begin to imagine what it would be like: gentle breezes, warm air, soft sand, the fragrance of tropical flowers, quiet relaxation, succulent fruits, spectacular sunsets. For people who don't like those things, there is no attraction. Perhaps what would attract them is a picture of a mountaintop with clear vistas, fresh air, the smell of pine trees, invigorating, crisp water from sparkling brooks, the call of birds, and the chatter of squirrels. Even if you hadn't planned on a trip, you might start planning what to pack. Pictures and visions create energy.

A common vision is vital because it represents hope. In Proverbs 29:18, we find an explanation for why a vision is necessary. Many nonprofit organizations find that their common vision of improving something brings people together, and they accomplish extraordinary things. Often the vision in nonprofit organizations is crystal clear to people who work there: well-fed children, healthy people, people with basic needs met, peace among people.

Someone once said that it is easy to understand the power generated by a vision. It is the difference between a flashlight and a laser. Both use a beam of light. The difference is that the beam of light from a flashlight is scattered in many directions, while the beam of light from a laser is aligned in one direction by a magnet. Both tools are useful. A laser will cut through obstacles, while a flashlight will simply highlight them. Energy and momentum are the products of desire. Set your sights on your desired future.

It is worthwhile to draw or paint an picture of what you hope to experience when you realize your vision. This book is critical to accomplishing my vision, which is inspired, joyful spirits thriving. That is my aim for you and me.

Mission

Mission is the overall reason for being and defines our distinctiveness. In his book *Quest for Quality in the Church: A New Paradigm,*[2] Ezra Earl Jones uses a wonderful description of how vision and mission fit together. He says that the vision is the picture within a frame, and the mission is the frame. The mission sets the boundaries within which we operate. He uses the example of Martin Luther King Jr., whose vision was so memorably described in his "I Have a Dream" speech—all people living together in peace. There are many missions that can lead to peaceful living for all. He chose civil rights as his mission.

Mission describe the field of endeavor. It defines what you will spend resources on as well as what you won't spend resources on. The word mission is not as important as clarifying the concept. It may be what you are called to do. I have spent much more time not writing this book than writing it. I realized that this is what I needed to do. The Choice Cycle was my assignment, my mission.

---

[2] Ezra Earl Jones.

I once had a horse with a crystal-clear vision and mission. Her name was Sweetheart, and she always knew what she would do and where she wanted to be. On any given day, I would put a bridle and saddle on her, and she would willingly let me ride her. We would go miles together until she decided that she was going home. No matter what I did, absolutely nothing that I tried stopped her from returning to the barn when she decided it was time. On the outbound journey, I was under the impression that I was in charge. It was only when my ideas of mission and vision differed from hers that it became apparent who was really in charge. There was something at the barn that Sweetheart valued more than the desire to be an agreeable horse.

Values

Values are the guiding principles and behaviors that embody how we operate. They are the background music and operating systems of our lives. Values reflect and reinforce the desired culture and support and guide our decisions. Clearly defined values make decision-making easier. As Walt Disney's nephew, Roy Disney, is widely quoted as saying, "When your values are clear to you, making decisions becomes easier." Or said in another way, "It's not hard to make decisions when you know what your values are."[3]

A common practice of adults is to ask a child, "What do you want to be when you grow up?" It appears to be a way to discuss vision, yet it strikes me as an odd way to make conversation with children. I think it is odd for a number of reasons. One is that children have very limited understanding of what is possible, and by the time they are adults, there will be infinitely more choices than at the current time. For example, children growing up in the 1950s could not have known that becoming a computer programmer was a possibility. Likewise, children of the 1970s would not likely wish to be a website designer. It is also a strange question because children (and adults) have a difficult time defining when one is actually a grown-up. Finally, time is an abstract concept to children.

I suggest that there are many better questions that could be framed in a time that is imaginable to a child and within their control. One such question could be "How do you want to act when you play with your friends?" or "What do you like to do?" Or perhaps "What do you want to be known for tomorrow?" or "Who do you want to be like and why?" Describing behavior sets an expectation of action rather than vision. To act in accordance with stated values means that the values are clear and a decision was made. The future will be, at least in part, a result of today's decisions.

Sometimes it is the questions that we ask of ourselves that define how we behave. Dr. David Morehouse[3] has spoken about how each of us has a perpetual question. When I heard him describe it, I knew exactly what he was talking about and what my perpetual question has been.

When I was four or five years old, my father went away to serve military duty and left my mother to care for my sister and me in a remote little village on the edge of the mountains, about fifteen miles from the nearest town. Late one evening, my mother, sister, and I returned to our home after dark, and there sitting in the middle of our yard was a big box with a new washing machine inside. It had been delivered. More to herself than to me or my sister, my mother said, "Now, how am I going to get that into the house?" In that instant, I heard my perpetual question, "How can I help?" It amazes me how clear the memory is and how clearly I remember my thought. I started thinking about how I could push it or try to lift it. Impossible tasks for a four-year-old. My soul, however, doesn't have an age or recognize physical limitations. It sees possibilities.

My perpetual question, "How can I help?" has had a huge influence on my life. My question has led me to my choice of college majors, careers, and friends. In many situations, I recognize that my desire to be helpful has driven my decisions and actions. It has driven me to teach, explain, and promote the Choice Cycle and to write this book.

It is very likely that you have your own story and perpetual question. Take a moment and reflect. What question do you hear you asking yourself, or in what situation do you place yourself so that you can get an answer or validation?

Your question and mine are just thoughts, and we can change them at any time. Indeed, there are questions that each of us should be asking ourselves each day. And those questions are not so different from the questions we ask children. For me and hopefully for you, the basis for the question is "How can I be better tomorrow than yesterday or today?" Because another moment is most likely coming, "How will I define the *me* of the next moments?"

---

[3] Roy Edward Disney was an American executive, son of Walt Disney's brother, Roy Oliver Disney (b.1930).
[4] Dr. Morehouse is an author and teacher of remote viewing, which is the practice of seeking impressions about a distant or unseen target using subjective means such as extrasensory perception (ESP).

Many years ago, I decided that I could define a few simple rules to live by. I began with an adaptation of a biblical scripture, Colossians 1:9–14.

To

- pray and ask God to fill me with knowledge of God's will through spiritual wisdom and understanding

In a way that I:

- live a life worthy of the Lord
- please my Creator in every way
- bear fruit in every good work
- grow in the knowledge of God
- am strengthened with all power

So that:

- I may have great endurance and patience
- I may joyfully give thanks to God, who has qualified me to share in the inheritance of the saints in the kingdom of light

I have regularly updated and transformed this into six values. I continue to adapt them because they help me stay focused and make difficult decisions.

I have learned that my rules need to be in place before I encounter moments when I need to make decisions. I need to be very clear on what I intend and why. Today, my values are the following:

- joy
- integrity
- faith
- peace
- nonviolence
- improvement

Constitutions

Groups, communities, and civilizations are created from shared or common interests and intentions. Collectively instructions, rules, visions, missions, and values could be called constitutions. Countries develop constitutions to define how they intend to act and govern themselves, because everybody acting on their own intentions would be chaotic and ineffective. Perhaps individuals can work alone with only intentions and intuition. To ensure groups are working together, constitutions are particularly important. Intuition is making choices on gut feel and guessing, without facts and without careful thought. Intuition is of limited value for groups or for individuals who intend to live consciously.

Organizations function best when the vision, mission, and values are written to be clear to all, shared and understood. Because they believe that it is important, many companies take time to create statements of their vision and mission and list their values. They may create documents and post them in the lobby of their buildings or put them on company literature and websites. Some companies never use them or refer to them after they are written. If they aren't used, it is very clear because decisions do not reflect what has been written. If not used, they can demotivate those who view them as platitudes or empty statements. To be useful, they must be memorable, simple, and visible, and visible means to be seen in actions. For the companies that do use them, they can be very powerful because they align the efforts of everyone involved in the enterprise.

There are many examples of mission and vision statements that were used with success. Here are two of my favorites. In 1962, John F. Kennedy, United States president, identified a mission to put a man on the moon by the end of the decade and return him safely to earth. In 1969, *Apollo 11* became the first spaceflight that landed humans on the moon, thus fulfilling the mission. In 1980, then Microsoft chairman and chief executive officer Bill Gates shared his vison to have a computer on every desk and in every home, running Microsoft software. Arguably, they have come close to achieving that vision. An example of clear values can be found in the Declaration of Independence of the United States. The founders of the United States declared what they believed were values worth fighting for—safety, security, life, liberty, and the pursuit of happiness.

Both missions and visons statements are statements of intentions. To be useful, however, intentions must be operational. A constitution is a way to make them operational and to describe a system. A system is a set of interconnected parts forming a complex whole with a purpose.[4]

Constitutions are used to establish *how* the governance of the system will work and define rights and responsibilities. To be effective, they have to be stable and flexible. Most countries have constitutions, but few individuals do. I decided that I could develop my own constitution. My constitution includes my vision, mission, and values. I make amendments whenever it needs to be improved or clarified or when my current constitution no longer serves my needs as a reliable guide.

Here are a couple examples of how I use my constitution:

1. Because I have decided that integrity is a value in my constitution, it includes honesty and guides my decisions. The decision is an easy one if I receive too much change or if someone makes an error in my favor. I simply return the excess. It is easy to call attention to the owner or return an item if I see someone drop something that belongs to them.
2. I chose improvement, and to me, that means to keep moving forward. A car that is not moving cannot be turned. In humans, paralysis (not moving) is often caused by fear. Improvement is choosing to reject fear and choosing to move forward. It is by moving forward that I have learned that joy comes after failure.

The primary difficulty is changing our way of thinking. There is no such thing as bad news. It means a shift to choose to see what might have been bad news, a failure, as an indicator to keep moving. If you're going through agony, keep going. It is not the time to stop. Begin the Choice Cycle again with the intent to learn.

---

[4] At the American Society for Quality's Annual Quality Congress in Philadelphia in 1998, the late Russell Ackoff, a professor at the Wharton School of Business at the University of Pennsylvania, described a system as a whole that consists of two or more parts and that the parts have three properties: 1) each part can affect the behavior or properties of the whole; 2) none of the essential parts can have an independent effect on the function of the whole; and 3) a combination of parts, or subsystem, has the same properties as the parts. The properties of the system are the product of the interaction of the parts, not the parts taken separately. Therefore, a system cannot be divided into independent parts. The performance of a system depends on how the parts interact, not on how the parts perform separately.

It is important to me to have and live with integrity, to constantly remember to maintain discipline and self-control over my mind, and to maintain the clarity provided by my personal constitution. Control over one's own thoughts is most likely a significant challenge for many of us. We can decide to increase our self-control and self-discipline and stay focused on our purpose. A guide to developing a personal constitution follows.

The Constitution of _____
Your name here

Definition of my constitution: The body of fundamental principles according to which I shall govern myself.

- *Purpose.* What is my fundamental reason for being? (I live to...)

  – _____

  – _____

- *Vision.* What is my picture of the future that will bring me joy to see?

- _____

- *Mission.* On what will I focus the use of my resources? _____

- *Values.* What will I use as the basis of my decisions? (I want to be known for...)

  – _____   _____   _____

  – _____   _____   _____

- *Beliefs.* Based on my experiences, what do I believe?

  – _____

  – _____

- *Code of Conduct.* What are rules that I intend to follow so that I will be both joyful and successful?

  – _____

  – _____

  – _____

  – _____

  – _____

Revised on _____
Date

33

The preamble of the US Constitution defines *why* the constitution was written. It includes "to form a more perfect union," "to establish justice," "to insure domestic tranquility," "to provide for the common defense," "to promote the general welfare," and "to secure the blessings of liberty."

Once completed, my constitution is useful only if I continually use it for guidance. Despite the fact that I had filled in all the blanks, I couldn't always recall the details, especially when I made revisions. I knew it would not be worth the time I had invested unless I used it every day. I printed it out and posted it in conspicuous places. I also put it on my cell phone so I could use it when I was out. I found that I needed to review and amend it based on experiences that I had or new things I learned. It can take any form that is useful to help you stay focused and disciplined.

Deciding *how* to use it was just the beginning. I needed to understand *why*. The why is the result that I want: integrity of mind, body, and soul; just, peaceful, secure, comfortable, and free. I love this definition of integrity that I heard: integrity is when all the parts touch.

Discipline

Without discipline, all of the intentions and written words are of no value. Discipline is the power to make our lives work as we intend. By living with discipline, we can identify what works, what doesn't work, and pay attention in the now. It isn't a power from outside ourselves, and it isn't a resource. It is power inside of ourselves. It is the power to trust that what we define in our constitution will help us live as we choose.

Sometimes people have a negative reaction to the word discipline because they associate it with punishment. They are not the same, however. Discipline is being focused and maintaining our direction.

A few years ago, I decided that I needed to improve my self-discipline. As a way to remind myself of that every day, I make my bed as soon as I got up. I make the bed even when I am at a hotel because I want to begin each day with discipline. It isn't an outward focus but rather an inward decision. Discipline teaches. Punishment does not. Punishment only demonstrates a power position. There is more information in chapter 8 about the dynamics of positions of power.

Lack of discipline leads to failure, and a return to discipline leads to joy because it helps us remember what we really want.

With my constitution defined and a commitment to maintain discipline, I realized that, just like the preamble, I needed to thoroughly understand my motivation.

CHAPTER 5

Drivers and Motivations—Why You Do What You Do

Management

The culture in which we live significantly influences what we do and why. I have lived all my life in the American culture and therefore have a built-in bias that sometimes seems like it is just part of the air that I breathe. In America (and I'm guessing other places as well), we love heroes. Action characters, sports stars, and rescuers make the headline news. Failures are also a popular topic in the media. In answer to a question about how to get media coverage for a quality improvement event, a local television station manager told me, "You can't. If it bleeds, it leads." It seems bad news is good for sales, and yet from my observations, there is more to it than that. It appears that many of the population in our culture have a serious type of drug addiction. That drug of choice is adrenalin, and many of us are hooked on thrills, be they large or small. We seek them and are adrenalin junkies. We need our fix.

I once worked in a job where one of my responsibilities was to notify customers of serious product problems. Whenever we received a customer complaint with severe consequences, my job was to convene a meeting of everyone involved in the decisions that needed to be made: recall the products, solicit more information from customers, and conduct an internal investigation. I felt good when I did a good job. I loved feeling important, and it was exciting to be involved in the crisis. One of my indicators that I was good at my job was that more than once customers called me and thanked me for notifying them of a recall. I loved my job because it was rewarding and important. Then I changed jobs and had

36

the same responsibilities but for a different product. The primary difference in the product lines was the severity of a product problem. In my new job, the consequences of a product problem would likely lead to deaths and life-threatening injuries. Now, as you might imagine, that company had very little interest in managing messes. I immediately noticed that I had no important meetings to arrange. The focus of my work shifted to doing everything we could to prevent problems. It wasn't long before I noticed that my phone didn't often ring. No urgent meetings. No calls from customers thanking me for the most recent recall notice. I found myself feeling depressed, as I didn't have emergency meetings to arrange, and I no longer felt important. That is when I realized that I missed the excitement of the old job and that I was hooked on the adrenalin that came from being on the front line and participating in the crises.

Prevention was not as personally rewarding to me, and I felt unimportant. While it might have looked bad to others, I quietly went about my work, teaching and evaluating what we had in place to prevent problems. I was not that visible and might have looked like a Maytag repairman[5] with no repairs to do. If the company was looking for ways to save money by eliminating nonvalue-adding activities, my quiet, nearly invisible activities could have meant the loss of my job.

I believe I actually went from a job in management to a job in leadership. I also believe that what motivates me to choose different roles is very common. What motivates me to play the role of manager is what is good for me (or my group). We could say that a recall is doing what is good for customers, but in reality, it is what will save the company lawsuits and more widespread negative publicity. What motivates me to play the role of leader is to think beyond myself or my group. It is making decisions based on what will be the greater good for everyone. If that is the motivation, then the choices will be to do whatever one can to prevent problems for ourselves and others.

Leadership

Someone once asked me to define the difference between leadership and management and to explain why I thought there are so few leaders. I remembered what it *felt* like when I changed jobs, and I think that is the essence of it. Leadership is not about being a hero or feeling important. It is about making

---

[5] A TV commercial by Maytag in 1967, bemoaning the fact that the Maytag repairman had nothing to do because the products were so reliable.

decisions differently, and it is not always the choice that feels good. Leaders can be lonely and are often targets of ridicule and derision. It is the difference between being good and looking good.

Leadership and management are a matter of perspective. It has been said that to someone with a new hammer, everything is a nail. The hammer is a weapon of power, and the nail is an object. Power is what, and the object is who.

Leadership and management are not roles so much as two different ways of seeing and behaving. They are often the product of habit or tradition. Leadership is internal power. Management is external power. Leadership is taking actions on the left side of the Choice Cycle, and management is taking actions on the right side.

I have found that when I choose to be a leader, I emphasize cooperation, and when I act as a manager, I focus on my competition. I can choose what is good for all, or I can choose what is good for me. If I am driven by caring and love, I am choosing a path of leadership, but when I am driven by my ego and feeling important, I am playing the role of manager.

Having said these things, let me be quick to add that we need both skills and roles. I think of leadership as preventing problems and management as fixing them. I very much believe in fire prevention, yet if my house is on fire, I want a firefighter! And I very much appreciate that when the fire alarm sounds and their adrenalin kicks in, they are available to save my house.

I am acting like a leader when my focus is:	I am acting like a manager when my focus is:
Community	Separation
Trust	Fear
Both/and	Either/or
Cooperation	Competition
Love	Ego
Good for all	Good for me
To be supportive	To be a hero

In response to "pay me now or pay me later" in a culture that thrives on excitement, it is often "I'll wait." I was reminded of this recently when a business owner told me that it was getting so difficult to make a profit that he had decided to stop doing quality control on his products. I thought, *Wow! That sounds like a very expensive decision*. It is expensive because the pay-me-later choice is *always* costlier.

It seems to me that dentistry is a profession that demonstrates leadership versus management as its premise. My reasoning is that the focus of good dentistry is to prevent cavities and to protect teeth from damage. Good oral hygiene is far from exciting; for those in the profession, it might be more exciting to find dental problems and fix them. Drill and fill could be more exciting than floss and brush. If I reasoned that floss, toothbrushes, and toothpaste were too expensive to buy regularly, then I might think I am saving money. When the pain comes, I will probably regret my shortsighted saving; however, fixing cavities, pulling teeth, and having a root canal are probably more expensive, both in cost and in pain.

Somewhere inside, we may fear that if we are effective at prevention, we will have nothing to do and no problems to address. In fact, dentistry proves that no matter how much we try to prevent trouble, there will always be failures. No matter how good our oral hygiene is, at some point we will probably still need a dental procedure to correct a problem.

The more we prevent and assess, the more resources we will have available to deal with the problems when they do arise, as they almost certainly will.

We can brush our teeth after meals, floss regularly, have sealant applied to our teeth, and follow dental hygiene instructions, yet we might still have a problem. We will discover it either by having professional cleaning and assessment or waiting until we feel pain or find evidence of a cavity. The sooner we find one cavity in a tooth, the less of our resources it will take, versus waiting until every tooth has cavities and some teeth can't be saved. I heard a dental hygienist say, "You don't have to floss all of your teeth. Just floss the ones you want to keep."

Likewise, you don't have to take time to pause or prevent. Just prevent things that you don't have the resources to manage. I remember talking to a business executive and telling him about a potential disaster with a new product introduction. I was shocked when he said, "Don't worry about it. I think we have the resources to manage it." Not surprisingly, the new product was indeed a disaster, and the resource that was depleted the most was the company's reputation. It never really recovered.

Whether we are called to the role of leader or manager, in order to be the best that we can be, we need to ensure that we are trained and prepared for what to expect. For leaders, it may be preparing for the lack of adrenalin. For managers, it may be participating in a simulation so that they are prepared for the real thing. Pilots practice flying in a simulator and experience challenges without having to actually fly and risk crash-landing an airplane.

Many years ago, I was working with a man whom I considered to be taking the actions of a true leader. He was speaking out against popular policies and working to reverse decade-old biased practices that were deemed acceptable and even normal to executives. I valued him and his leadership, and from my experience with the Choice Cycle, I knew that what he was doing was high risk. He was doing what he believed was right (good for all), not what was popular (good for him, his career, and his group). I decided there was something I could do, so I set up a meeting with him and shared the Choice Cycle with him. I told him that I and many others appreciated what he was doing and that we knew that he would get no rewards from the established system that he was trying to improve. I invested my time, energy, and knowledge to help empower a true leader. Leaders can be lonely and feel isolated. It is not unlike winning the game being played in the visitor's territory. Leaders need to know that they are not alone. Leadership is risky. In his book *Leadership without Easy Answers*, Harvard professor and founding director of the Center for Public Leadership at the John F. Kennedy School of Government, Ronald A. Heifetz, entitled one chapter "Assassination." That is one of the risks of leadership. It may not always be physical assassination. It might be political or career assassination. I believe that leaders do what they do because of an internal drive or set of values and beliefs, and it is often seen as counterculture. Managers may be driven by commonly accepted external motivators, and what is common is often seen as normal.

Another way to say it is leaders seek wyn/win. Wait! Before you think that's a typo, recognize that even though I think that those who have only one way to spell a word lack creativity, I do use spellcheck. Wyn/win stands for What You Need *before* What I Need. It is not instead of, just a way to remember the order of priorities. It is still win-win which should be the goal. The win-lose scenario, competition, is an unsustainable transitional status. It is usually on the way to lose-lose. True leaders seek win-win, and managers often seek to beat the competition. Managers want to win, and they want their competition to lose. Sadly, this is often the way politics operates. The goal appears to be a competition to create of winners and losers.

Sometimes we hear stories of high-profile people doing what the rest of us believe is foolish. It happens in politics, sports, business, and probably every endeavor that involves humans making decisions regarding their own behavior. Although it probably isn't a conscious thought, they may be motivated by the need of an adrenalin fix. It explains the behavior of people who lack personal challenges of everyday life. If we were chauffeured everywhere, managed down to the microsecond, and lacked the challenges of choosing what to wear, any of us might choose to participate in clandestine activities just for the thrills. It is at the heart of scandals. Of course, there is often an accompanying belief that their private failure will not become a public failure. By understanding the Choice Cycle, we know that it is just a matter of time until what is done in secret becomes public knowledge. The cost of trying to manage public failure and thereby avoiding confession can be infinite. Despite their belief in their own power, influence, and financial resources, those who make such choices to gamble and risk often learn that they do not have enough resources and that awareness of the failure is out of their control. Time moves forward, and given time, all of the seeds of failure yield a bountiful harvest.

Leadership and management are a matter of give and take. Leadership gives, and management takes. It all works well if leaders give what they can and managers take only what they need. Like balancing a checking account, balance is key.

CHAPTER 6

Trade-Offs—Choosing Balance

As we walk, we move between two steady states—dynamic and static. Likewise, when we breathe, we shift between inhalation and exhalation. At that moment in between, we pause. Unless we are concentrating on it, we don't even recognize the pause. And just as in the Choice Cycle, it is that pause at the transition point that keeps us balanced.

When we walk and breathe, we typically don't think that we are making a decision to maintain our balance, but we are.

When we recognize the need for a resource that we do not have, we often try to use one resource that we do have to make up for the lack of another. Money may be used to buy influence. Stuff may be used to get money. Relationships may be used to buy time. I heard someone say of a large corporation, "When they have a problem, they throw money on it until they can't see the problem anymore." When we have a need, we often begin to take an inventory or account of our assets and means. We identify the possible sources and reserves that we can use.

Priorities

A couple stories from my experience may illustrate this best.

Money

It was the kind of news I didn't want to hear. The cost of the after-school care program was going to almost double. I began to think of alternatives. Perhaps my daughter was old enough to stay at home alone. A few days later, I met a woman whom I judged to be a bit coarse. She just had a hard way about her. We were in a group growth session together, and I was shocked when she shared her story. She recounted that when she was about the same age as my daughter, she was brutally attacked on her way home from school. Suddenly I saw this woman as a courageous soul for sharing her story and for her endurance and survival. I also realized what a terrible cost of failure could be. Suddenly, the increased cost of safe after-school care seemed like an incredible bargain.

Time

A man with whom I worked was bragging that he never takes a vacation because his job is his first priority. Later in the conversation, he complained that his six-year-old son bugs him every day to play catch and that he just doesn't have the time. When I had the opportunity, I said, "You know, your son will get your attention. It is a case of pay me now or pay me later. You can play catch with him now (prevention) or wait until he is a troubled teenager, and you'll spend ten times more time and a lot of money and energy (public failure)." It's a choice. I don't know if he chose to accept my advice or not. It would take many years for the results to become clear.

Prevention can seem very expensive if you don't calculate the cost of failure. I hear people say, "Well, it is a calculated risk." I am tempted to reply, "Show me your calculations." What they really mean is "I'll take a chance."

It is always a challenge to find the right balance for deciding and using resources. It is helpful to have clearly defined intentions. Another way to choose is to calculate the cost of a potential failure. If you are willing to pay the price, then you can decide to wait or decide that you can bear the pain, cost, and embarrassment of public failure.

Road Maps

Road maps can be very useful to help us get where we want to go. They aren't so helpful, however, if you don't know where you are and where you want to go. We rarely make decisions based on what resources we have. I don't plan my trip by just looking at the gas gauge and deciding that I'll go until I run out of fuel. I usually plan my destination first. Then I choose the direction, and then I make sure I have the resources I need. When I come to a fork in the road, I have anticipated that there will be points where I must make a good decision. The map helps me anticipate when I need to be ready.

We don't often do the same with life decisions, but there are some things we can anticipate. Remember the simulators that pilots use. We can prepare ourselves for decisions. Looking at the Choice Cycle, we notice that the expenditure of resources is heavily weighted on the right, managing failures. If we believe that nothing will happen that we need to manage, we are fooling ourselves. Conventional wisdom tells us to save for a rainy day. That's not bad advice, except that it leads us to believe that amassing resources is the most important thing to do.

Let's face it; all of our resources are important, and we want to make the best decisions we can to make the most of them. Sometimes I have found that it is easier to make decisions by just figuring out where I am in the cycle. Knowing it is the part of the cycle that is repetitive, I can anticipate what is coming next. I have a chance to determine if I have the resources that I need for the journey and to anticipate possible problems and prepare for them.

I need to get my thinking balanced so that my resources will be balanced. I need to do all I can to prevent problems, so I need to invest as many resources as I can in prevention. As an investment for the future, I need to learn as much as I can. When I am as prepared as I can be, then I make the decision to go and accomplish what I am prepared to do. I then can ask, "How did it go?" I can ask myself, and I can ask others who were impacted by my actions. I gather as much information as I can, which, of course, will be another investment. The sooner I know whether it worked or not, the fewer resources I need. After I ask, I can classify the results as success or failure. Now I know, so it is a private failure. Now the best decision I can make is to get through it as fast as I can. Make it public and move on.

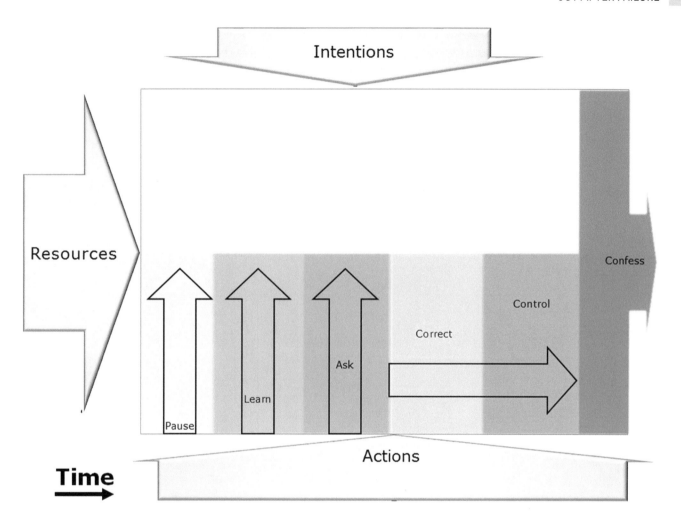

The pattern is to use as many resources as you can for preparation, prevention, and assessment. Then when you know that there is a failure, get through it as fast as you can.

When we make decisions based *only* on resources, it is almost a guarantee that it will eventually be considered a bad decision. That is because by eliminating spending efforts on preparation, prevention, and assessment, the only thing left is failure.

Figure 1 shows what happens when we decide to reduce budgets by a percentage or try to save the resources by shaving expenditures across all actions. It is a decision that first eliminates pausing.

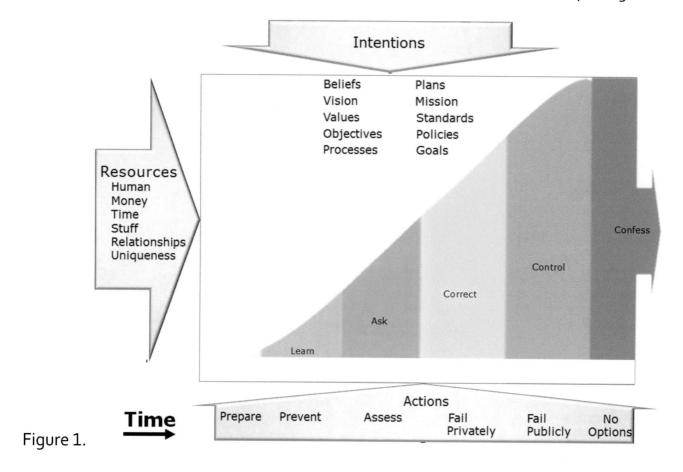

Figure 1.

Figure 2 illustrates what happens when we decide to further reduce resources. Learning is eliminated. Often, training and development budgets are some of the first reductions.

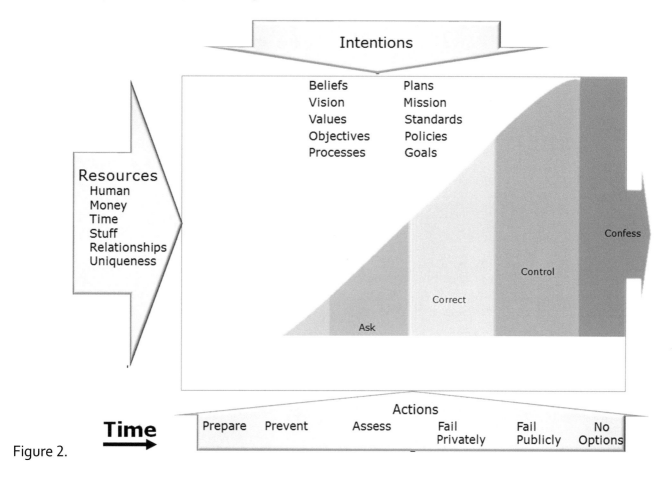

Figure 2.

Figure 3 depicts what happens when we continue to reduce resources. We don't do assessments or even ask or try to learn.

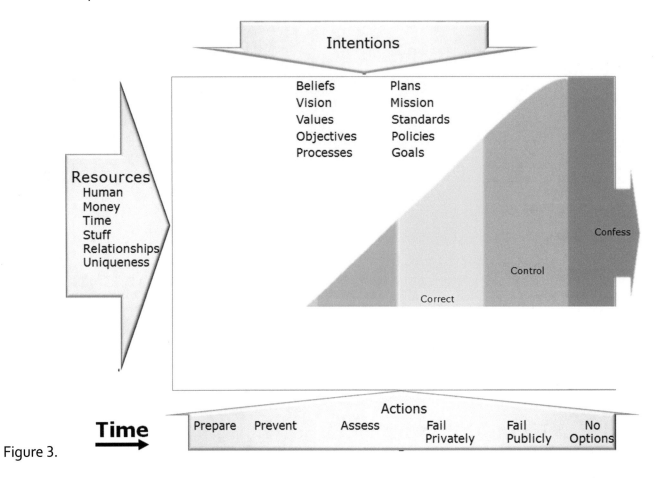

Figure 3.

Figure 4 shows what happens when we continue to decrease expenditures. The actions that are left are managing failures, and eventually the only action left is to confess.

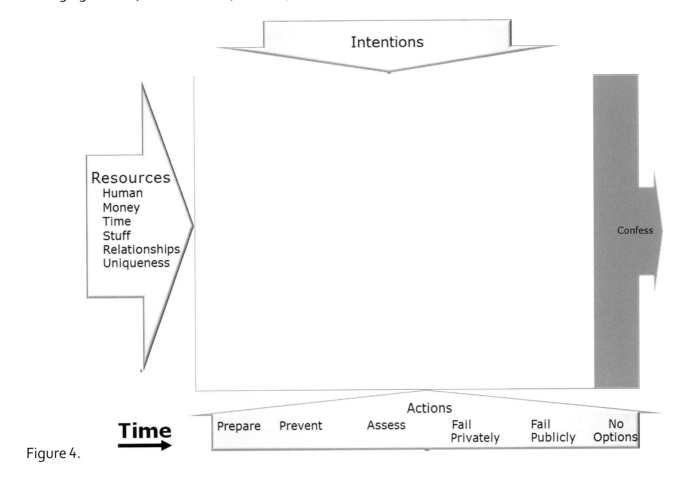

Figure 4.

This kind of decision-making is common in businesses and organizations that are focused only on the bottom line. One of the ways to recognize businesses that are focused on money is to watch what they do in difficult financial times. Do they downsize the workforce? Do they sell assets? Do they cut the budgets for training or quality testing and audits? Some managers say they don't train people because it is an investment—and what if they leave? A friend of mine is fond of responding, "What will it cost if you don't train them and they stay?"

Some people are focused on money, and many of their decisions are driven by their affection for money. The real choices are made moment by moment, and the choices are constant. There is no choice except now or later. Later is *always* more expensive.

It is helpful to use the Choice Cycle to answer the questions we ask ourselves: How? What? Why? It has been said that what is most often missing in businesses and in our lives is the *why*. Intention first, then which actions and when to take them, and finally how to get the resources needed. If we start with how, we will deprive ourselves of balance and joy. It takes self-discipline to maintain a focus on intention.

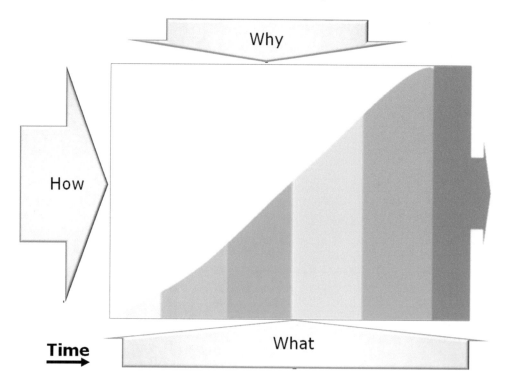

From another perspective, the need for balance is easier to visualize. Looking at the Choice Cycle from the point of view of intentions demonstrates how important it is to stay centered. Peace is at the center, and the more resources we spend, the further we are from balance. Spending resources on managing failures leads to burnout.

CHAPTER 7

Being a Phoenix—Rising from the Ashes of Failure

Life goes on even when we don't believe that it will and when we may not even want it to. We may desire an end to this, whatever "it" is, and it does end. Nothing lasts forever, neither the good times nor the bad ones.

One of my favorite activities is taking photographs of flowers. I have found such beauty and enjoyment in noticing the flowers and capturing the images. Yet there is one thing that I absolutely know. As you read this, not one of the flowers that I have photographed still exists today. They, like all of life, returned to the earth from which they drew life. Nature is a wonderful teacher about cycles. In nature, the cycle is that after death, the flower will decompose and become a resource for something else. We have an opportunity following failure—the end, death—to choose how our resources will be used *next time*. The remnants, residue, and ashes fuel and feed what comes next. We take the pain, the embarrassment, the frustrations, and debris and decide how to use it, learn from it, and recycle it into a new future. We can create a future that is filled with hope, dreams, and opportunities. We rise from the ashes and begin again—perhaps wiser, perhaps more intentional, and perhaps more focused but certainly not exactly the same. I once saw a sign on someone's desk that said, "Sometimes you win, and sometimes you learn." True failure is wasting an opportunity to learn and rethink, and even then, we may have an opportunity to begin anew. The debris of death in one cycle brings energy to the next life. Organic matter breaks down and becomes oil and carbon, and with time, pressure, and heat, it may become diamonds. Change is inevitable.

We fall, we falter, and we fail. Clichés tell us our experiences are not unique. We aren't the only ones. The world keeps turning; time marches on; we pick ourselves up, dust ourselves off, and start all over again.[6] I once heard someone say, "Fall down and get up is one step." It takes resources like courage and resolve. When we are feeling like life is hard, imagine hard life experiences as seeds. Seeds must be broken open to take root. Like flowers, new ideas, dreams, hopes, and babies begin as seedlings or *startlings* (new starts). They are fragile, tender, and in need of protection, shelter, gentle treatment, water, and nourishment. Given an appropriate environment, all will be fruitful. They all need an environment that meets their needs without restrictions, violence, or smothering.

The environment that is created is not always from the outside. Our own self-talk can be a key part of our environment. What we say to ourselves can be gentle or violent. Next time is gentle, and we give ourselves a choice to learn. Saying to ourselves, "I should not have done that," or "I failed," is not creating a safe space. Correction and discipline can be gentle. Criticism is not. Name-calling is neither gentle nor helpful. Startlings need time and patience, not forcing. Everything is a process. We begin, we try, we learn, and begin again.

Life often offers and presents opportunities many times until we finally learn. When we haven't succeeded, it just means that success hasn't happened yet. We didn't decide incorrectly. It's just that we haven't completed the lesson.

Words can be inflammatory and signal a coming explosion. "That really burns me up." "He/she/it kills me." "I've had enough." "That's it." Listen carefully. Failures are cleverly disguised opportunities for growth. After a forest fire, the affected area goes through many changes, and new growth begins and flourishes.

What we can do is create the atmosphere and environment that nurtures the next cycle—be it a minute, a day, a week, a month, a year, or a life experience. After a failure, it is so easy to try to blame others and not examine how we contributed to the failure. We fail to see it from a different point of view. Using hurtful words and inflicting pain does nothing to lessen any of the damage. Whatever has happened is over. Nothing will make it different from what it is. It is too late to prevent anything. Sometimes we beat

---

6   A line from the song "Pick Myself Up" that was sung by Fred Astaire and Ginger Rogers in the Depression-era movie *Swing Time*.

ourselves up, and that doesn't help. What does help is focusing forward and finding what can prevent it from happening again. When used properly, ashes make a great medium for growth.

As a tired parent, I picked up my child after school, and after a thirty-minute drive, we were almost home. That is when my child realized that she had left her coat on the playground at the school. *Aha,* I thought. *It's a public failure and time for a choice of what I can control.* We used the time going back to the school to focus on prevention. We both tried to think of as many ways as we could for her to remember her coat. Neither of us were left feeling bad, and we were both engaged in planning for the next time. I could have become angry and berated her, which would have depleted both of our energy resources. It was a wise investment. By focusing on next time, together we found a better way to use our resources, energy, and time. Further, we created joy.

Recently, I had the experience of looking at a calm ocean, and it looked uniform from the surface. When I was airborne over the same ocean, with distance and a view from high above it, I could see patterns, waves, currents, and underwater plants growing. The same is true of situations. Wonderful things can happen when we choose to see from a different perspective.

I once saw a definition of nagging that sounds different from how I had defined it: to find fault incessantly; to complain, to be a persistent source of annoyance or distraction; to irritate by constant scolding or urging. It was that last word that got my attention. I had never thought of urging as nagging. I had thought of it as encouragement, but it is a distraction. Persistent urging draws attention. It is not unlike the distraction of a constantly barking dog. Moment by moment, the noise can drown out our inner voice, intentions, plans, and purpose. The urging voice says, "Listen to me. Pay attention to me. Do as I suggest. What's important is my view, my desire, and my idea."

Theodore Roosevelt said, "It is not the critic who counts; not the man who points out how the strong man stumbles, or where the doer of deeds could have done them better. The credit belongs to the man who is actually in the arena; whose face is marred by dust and sweat and blood; who strives valiantly; who errs and comes up short again and again; who knows the great enthusiasms, the great devotions, and spends himself in a worthy cause; who, at best, knows in the end the triumph of high achievement; and who, at worst, if he fails, at least fails while daring greatly, so that his place shall never be with those cold and timid souls who know neither victory nor defeat."

Instead of urging or criticizing, let them do and choose what they choose. It is their Choice Cycle and their lesson to learn.

Nagging is as if, in the beginning of the relationship, each participant begins with a supply of salt. As the relationship begins, it grows and takes root in a combined soil of traditions and expectations. They each bring legacies that may be healthy or not. To help the other, one of the participants urges actions. The participants enrich the soil of the relationship with a grain of salt. The other may not notice or may not even mind. Each time urging adds a little or a lot of salt. As it continues, the relationship begins to show signs of disease. (Disease is a state of uneasiness as well as sickness.) If salt is added until the roots can take no more, they die. Death of a relationship is a public failure that most of us have experienced at least once, and some of us have experienced it repeatedly.

The prefix *dis* means apart or not, so it changes the meaning of words to the opposite. Failure then is the opposite of what we want. Failure to be at ease becomes disease. Comfort becomes discomfort. Courage becomes discourage.

After public failure, it is once again a choice to pause and consider what caused the opposite of what we wanted. There is an opportunity to learn and to do what it takes to prevent a repeat and fatal disease. Wisdom is learning the power of a grain of salt.

There is a wonderful work by Portia Nelson entitled *Autobiography in Five Short Chapters*. It tells a wonderful tale of learning from experiencing failures. I highly recommend reading it and learning its lessons well. It is widely available on the internet.

This chapter could have a theme song.

From *Zootopia*, this is "Try Everything":

I messed up tonight
I lost another fight
I still mess up but I'll just start again
I keep falling down
I keep on hitting the ground

I always get up now to see what's next
Birds don't just fly
They fall down and get up ...

At the end of each day, find something to celebrate. We need to hold ourselves accountable and be proud of our choices. Giving thanks and gratitude are a great start of the next Choice Cycle. Joy is in appreciating what we have. Our lives and joy are the sum total of our choices.

CHAPTER 8

*Joy in Your Future Is Your Choice—
What Will Your Perspective Be?*

When we believe that one of our resources is more important than others, it drives our decisions. We can dramatically increase one of our resources by simply changing the way we think. Joy is a product of perspective—a state of mind and being. Joy doesn't depend on circumstances. It is free from constraints, and often it is our thoughts that create our circumstances. Thought is independent of resources. Our thoughts are our choice. We choose to think what we think. Some resources are limited, and some are unlimited. Some are tangible or material, and some are intangible or spiritual. Relationships can be unlimited. Relationships are the result of thoughts, beliefs, and attitudes.

One-Up/One-Down

Many years ago, Janice Eddy, a management and diversity consultant and author, introduced me to the concept of one-up/one-down. Because I understand better by seeing pictures, I developed this model to help me visualize it.

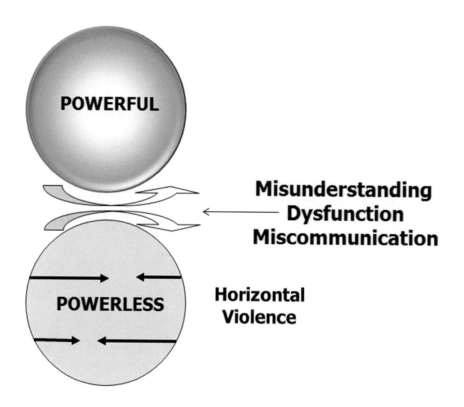

It shows the dynamics of relationships. It is a model of attitudes in action. One-up is experienced as powerful, and one-down is experienced as powerless. We are believed to be or claim to be one-up based on any of a whole host of things, such as race, gender, age, finances, position, or status. One-up is an experience of having power or privilege, such as being rich, young, male, white, executive, a supervisor, or boss. One-down is an experience of being powerless or disadvantaged, such as poor, elderly, female, nonwhite, worker, servant.

A one-up can be an oppressor to the one-down: victor and victim; hunter and hunted; stalker and prey; haves and have-nots; insider and outsider; member and visitor; bully and target. No matter what the circumstances, it is an interaction that involves both energy and fear.

Typically, the one-downs want the relationship to change, and the one-ups want to maintain status quo. The vision of how things could be creates energy for one-downs, and that energy does not impact the power. It often appears to be a case of an unstoppable force meeting an immovable object. The energy is kinetic and has to go somewhere, so it turns into horizontal violence. Horizontal violence is hostility, aggression, and harmful behavior. The term is most often used in reference to the nursing profession. In a culture where there is a group that is often seen as powerful, doctors, and other groups seen as powerless, the powerless turn on one another. Nurses turn on other nurses, nurses turn on lab techs, lab techs pick on food service workers, housekeeping workers complain about (fill in the blank). This dynamic happens far beyond one profession. It is powerful and is widely demonstrated. It is rich-powerful and poor-powerless. It is Caucasians-powerful and people of color–powerless. So begins conflicts—gangs fighting with each other, sibling rivalry, black-on-black crime, and race wars.

To be one-up is to be numb, even clueless. One-up/one-down is subtle. Typically, one-down is the first to notice the nature of the relationship. If we are a one-up, we can be unaware or deny that there even *is* a one-down. Whether conscious or not, our efforts are to stay one-up. In order to maintain one-up, we can switch between "I know it all" and "I don't know anything about it." The result is choosing to be unaware, blind, and deaf to the experiences and the plights of others. When we are one-down, our life or safety depends on understanding those who are one-up. The result is awareness, seeing, and hearing. It is interesting that one-ups believe that they understand everything when quite the opposite is true. Wisdom comes easiest from being one-down.

Perspective

Smart is not the same as wise. There is a wonderful children's book entitled *Seven Blind Mice* by illustrator, author, and Caldecott Medalist Ed Young. It is a tale of trying to describe something from a limited point of view. Spoiler alert. His final pages say, "Seeing in part makes a great tale, but wisdom comes from seeing the whole." One-up is wanting more and never being satisfied. One-down is needing and not getting enough. By understanding and cooperating, we reach a balanced whole. Joy comes from seeing, valuing, and caring for the whole.

One-ups may even express empathy for one-downs, but they are not willing to give up their own power. The source of their power is from the one-downs. Without one-downs, there are no one-ups. One-ups pull power all the while talking about wanting to empower the one-downs. They may speak of wanting to empower others yet hold on to their power position.

The basis for that fear in one-ups is likely that they believe that if they were to become one-down, they would be invisible, treated poorly, or disregarded, the very way that they treat one-downs. One-ups and one-downs never share the same experience even though they have been through the same events.

The dysfunction and failures come because there is no real communication. They talk at each other or about each other without a desire to learn. Because the one-ups are unaware or dismissive of one-downs, they continue to ignore reality. Effective solutions must come from the one-downs because they understand the issues as well as the dynamics of reality. The lack of effective communication, misunderstanding, lack of respect, and comparisons are underlying causes.

The one-downs recognize the issues that plague the one-ups and even try to help them or bring attention to those in power. In spite of inadequate understanding or a very limited perspective, one-ups may offer suggestions, answers, or fixes and expect solutions or improvements to be done by the one-downs. Suggestions from the one-downs are ignored or deemed impractical.

Maintaining one-up/one-down positions prevents real relationships. They remain in those positions as long as the one-up's power is allowed and the one-down's powerlessness is accepted. A new dynamic requires changes that are often not welcome or embraced. Status quo is often less painful than change. It requires a shift from *they* to *we*. It takes an acknowledgment that both are responsible. We are all responsible for the dynamics of relationships.

Because the interactions are based on attitude, they can change. No one is actually one-up or one-down. None of us is any better or any worse than any of the rest of us. It is a choice to compare, and it is always possible to find attitudes of superiority and inferiority. Comparison is a problem because it brings in distraction, disappointment, and depression. They are states of disease.

One thing that helps to bring about a change is trying a different point of view. Put things in a bigger context. In the view of earth from the moon, people appear to be equal, which, in reality, is what we are. One-ups tend to focus on power (the what). One-downs tend to focus on people (the who).

One way to recognize the one-up attitude is by checking yourself for prejudice. The difference in prejudice and conviction is that conviction can be stated without anger.

Change

One-ups see the world as a mountain or pyramid. For example, for many men, success is about getting to the top, and failure is being somewhere in the middle. One-downs see the world as a wheel. For many women, success is being in the center, and failure is being on the outside. Boys are said to play king of the mountain, and girls play house. Boys' games are often battles, and girls' games are often relationships.

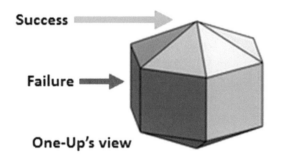

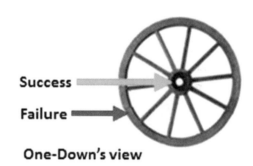

It is a matter of perspective. If you view the pyramid from a point high above, the top is the center, but for a one-down, it feels like being an outsider. For a one-up, their feeling of failure is the same point as the one-down's feeling of success.

To change the dynamic and begin a transition and move from dysfunctional to functional requires disciplined thinking, a shared desire for change, and trust. When the dynamic begins to shift, it may feel like a free fall or failure to one-ups. It might also feel like one-ups are being forced. To reach equality is a relationship in balance, but the parties' common goal must be being compatible, which takes coordination and cooperation.

Effective Interactions

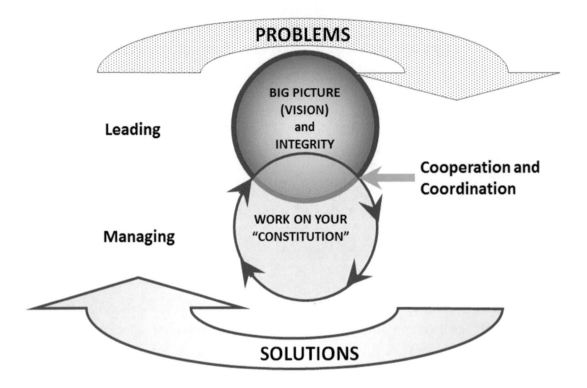

If a one-up and one-down honestly decide to try to understand each other, a connection can be made. Connections matter. On a tombstone, there are often two dates, the birth and death. Between the beginning and the end is a dash. What really matters is the dash that connects them because the dash represents the life.

There is hope. We can thoughtfully make connections and cooperate. We can change and have new experiences that will result in joy. We can evolve into better relationships. We can follow a journey from considering only me to recognizing when we are acting out the dynamics of either one-up or one-down to cooperating in improving alignment and finally being in close alignment. We think more alike than different.

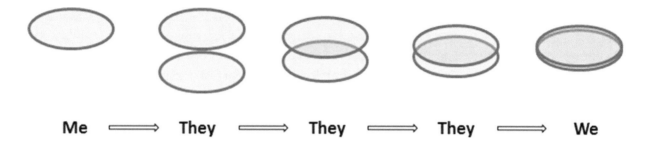

Me $\Longrightarrow$ They $\Longrightarrow$ They $\Longrightarrow$ They $\Longrightarrow$ We

Disciplining our thinking is sometimes the greatest challenge. I like to think of it as replacement therapy.

- Replace lusting with honesty.
- Replace excess with fairness and restraint.
- Replace greed with generosity.
- Replace laziness with persistence and enthusiasm.
- Replace anger with patience and peacefulness.
- Replace envy and comparison with satisfaction and kindness.
- Replace self-pride with humility and modesty.
- Replace opinions and information with knowledge, understanding, and wisdom.

All of us have opinions. Information can be found in books. None of us have all knowledge or perfect understanding or are wise in all things. If we seek knowledge—seek to really understand—and desire wisdom, we can learn.

Learning is the beginning of the Choice Cycle.

Awareness is possible any time we decide to wake up. It is when we are wide awake that everything seems different. It's an instantaneous choice. I can move down a path or drive down a road and be completely distracted by thoughts that have nothing to do with the present moment, or I can move along, focused on how light filters in or how it illuminates a leaf, a blade of grass, or a flower.

Likewise, I can eat a meal or consume a beverage, or I can slow down or awaken to the moment and taste, feel the texture, and savor the flavor. I can become aware of how long the flavor and aroma linger. What changed is me. Staying awake takes a lot of effort, but we can do it.

Wyn/Win

There are no villains or heroes in this. We need to share the mission of seeking the greater good. In his book *Lila: An Inquiry into Morals*, author and philosopher Robert M. Pirsig describes sorting ideas recorded on index cards. Some did not seem to belong to any category. He stated, "These were the underdogs, the outsiders, the pariahs, the sinners of the system." But the reason he was so concerned about them was that he felt the quality and strength of his entire system of organization depended on how he treated them. If he treated the pariahs well he would have a good system. If he treated them badly he would have a weak one.

What would it look like if we decided to identify consistently *and* accommodate the needs of one-downs? The identification should be easy. If we listen to the rhetoric, we will hear someone referred to as "they." One-ups are those without disadvantages (or so they think). For example, if a one-up is an able-bodied person, a one-down would be someone who is physically challenged. Their challenge could be mobility, hearing, seeing, or smelling. If we chose to adapt the system of public access for one-downs with mobility challenges, we would need to wake up and see the barriers: stairs, curbs, inaccessible seating, and unreachable areas. It would mean working to eliminate barriers. It would mean installing elevators, sloped sidewalks, low door thresholds, and ramps. And our culture did that. Did it improve life for the one-downs? Yes. Did it weaken the system for the one-ups? No. In fact, the one-ups benefit also. They can use luggage with wheels, easily move objects on carts, and use automatic doors when their hands are full. There is a law called Americans with Disabilities Act (ADA) that is administered by the Department of Justice (interesting!) that defines standards for creating improved access. Those things that eliminated barriers are used and appreciated by everyone. It has improved the quality and strength of our system. "And justice for all" became more of a reality. It is a great possibility if we choose wyn/win. That is taking care of someone else's need before I get what I need. See chapter 5.

There is a proverb that states that it is impossible to wake up someone who is pretending to be asleep. Said another way, ignorance is an option. When we awaken to the disabling dynamic relationships created by acting as if there is a one-up or one-down, we end our ignorance. Author and illustrator Don Wood stated, "Stupid is forever, but ignorance can be fixed." Ignorance is defined as being unaware. Stupid is "not intelligent, careless, having or showing the lack of ability to learn." The root word for stupid comes from a Latin adjective that means amazed or stunned. Because a one-up is numb, everything outside of their experience is stunning. Ending the numbness would mean an awakening.

If we wake up, we become aware of our biases, prejudices, and assumptions. We can end our own self-centeredness and our desire to stay one-up because we discover the high cost of ignorance.

The end of one-up/one-down is the beginning of a world that works better for everyone. If we listen (with all our senses), we can learn. We can eliminate ignorance (ignoring reality). We can't say, "I didn't know." Yes, we did. I love the way Harper Lee said it through Atticus Finch in *To Kill a Mockingbird*, "You never really understand a person until you consider things from his point of view—until you climb into his skin and walk around in it."

Sometimes we can feel very connected or even controlled by how we think of money. When we see it as *the* primary resource, we give it power over our decisions. When we see it as just one of our many resources, it can feel less important. We distinguish the difference between money and wealth because they are not the same. Feeling wealthy is similar to feeling joy. It takes into consideration all of our resources. We can be wealthy and have very little money. Conversely, we can have plenty of money and be impoverished or depleted. To be wealthy means having more than a lot of money or stuff. Wealthy is freedom from wanting more. Wanting less can lead to more joy. We can want less if we focus on what we have rather than what we don't have. We are aware of what we don't have when we compare with others.

Want and need are also very different. What we need sustains our lives: water, air, nutrients, and sleep. What we want does not sustain, and it can even destroy our joy. More want, less joy. We have to be careful to not convince ourselves that what we want is what we need.

We are satisfied when what we expect is what we actually get. We can choose and be satisfied with what we actually have and eliminate expectations. Satisfaction makes us wealthy and can lead to joy.

Power and force are not the same. Force is an actual physical phenomenon, and power is not physical. Technically, power is an expression of energy, and force is an interaction between two objects.

Kinetic energy is movement/work and is dynamic. Potential energy is static and is related to position. The late Lou Tice was cofounder of the Pacific Institute, an education company that teaches individuals and organizations to fulfil their potential. He described someone as "so powerful he could be gentle."

We need to understand that being forceful is not the same as being powerful. Too often, the words are used interchangeably. Powerful people are leaders who use their resources for the good of all.

Together

We are in it together and are responsible for the status and the changes that are needed. To improve our lives and the choices we make, we must wake up. We can help one another. Together in a healthy relationship, we are wealthy. That is the wonderful thing about failure; it wakes us up. That is when we have an opportunity to change old habits and end old prejudice. The beginning of joy is pausing to consider what matters to you, learning from mistakes and failures, and then giving it a go. We know that we will all fail and succeed. Failure is not the opposite of success. Failure is a necessary event that will position you on the path to success. What follows failures is joy. Someone once said, JOY is putting *Jesus* first, *Others* second, and *Yourself* last. In other words, put the priority on faith. Joy is after being numbed by failures and now being awake, for having a plan and good intentions and knowing how to make decisions to get there.

I once saw a sign on a muddy Alaskan road that said, "Choose your rut carefully. You will be in it for the next 200 miles."

The Choice Cycle is our way out of our rut.

ABOUT THE AUTHOR

Linda grew up in a small rural community, graduated from college, and began working in health care, a career that she loved. Professional adventures took her through careers in medical devices, quality management, customer service, auditing, consulting, and the hospitality industry.

For more than forty years, she has enjoyed leading, coaching, consulting, teaching, and writing to help a wide variety of individuals and organizations succeed, grow, and prosper. During that time she has shared The Choice Cycle with thousands of people in classes, seminars and conferences and has always looked forward to providing it to a larger audience.

Her passion is helping people, teams, and groups create methods and systems to sustain excellence. She has lived in Colorado, California, and Delaware and now lives in North Carolina.

She loves books and has wanted to write her own for a long time. This is the fulfillment of that dream.

Printed in the United States
By Bookmasters